Sad

By Janine Amos
Illustrated by Gwen Green

CHERRYTREE BOOKS

Sad

A CHERRYTREE BOOK

This edition first published in 2007
by Cherrytree Books, part of
The Evans Publishing Group Limited
2A Portman Mansions
Chiltern St
London
W1U 6NR

British Library Cataloguing in Publication Data

Amos, Janine
Sad. - 2nd ed. - (Feelings)
1. Sadness - Juvenile literature 2. Melancholy - Juvenile literature
I. Title
155.4'124

ISBN 9781842344798
First published in paperback1997

CREDITS
Editor: Louise John
Designer: D. R. ink
Production: Jenny Mulvanny

Karen's story

Karen sat up in bed and looked at the clock. It was almost eight!

"Today's the day," she thought. "I mustn't be late." Karen had been waiting for this day for weeks. Her teacher was getting married – and Karen's whole class was invited to the wedding!

Just then, Karen's mum came into the bedroom.

"Hurry up, Karen," she said, smiling. "Today's the day!" Karen's mum pulled open the curtains. Then she turned round and stared at Karen's face.

"Oh, no!" said Karen's mum.

"What?" asked Karen. "There's nothing wrong."

"Oh yes there is," said her mum. "You can't go. Look at yourself."

Karen looked in the mirror. One side of her face had puffed out into a huge lump.

"It's mumps," said Karen's mum. "The swelling will go in about a week. Now you get back into bed and I'll bring you some juice."

Karen got back into bed and lay down. She looked at the sun shining outside. She looked at her new dress hanging carefully over the chair. And she thought about all the other children at Miss Kane's wedding.

How do you think Karen felt?

Karen's head ached. Her throat was sore and she was very hot. "Mumps, I hate you," she thought.

When Karen's mum came back, Karen sat up in bed.
"Please let me go, Mum. I feel fine!" she said.
"No, Karen. You might pass on mumps to someone else," said her mum.
"But I have to give Miss Kane the posy," said Karen.
"One of your friends will do it," said her mum.

Karen's sister Marie came in.

"I can't go to the wedding," Karen told her.

"Weddings are silly, anyway!" said Marie. "Let's play a game. Let's play I-Spy."

"Oh, get lost, Marie!" snapped Karen.

Marie went away and Karen's eyes filled up with tears.

"No one understands," she thought.

Why is Karen upset with Marie?

After a while Karen got up. She tiptoed over to the chair and put on her new dress. She pulled on her tights and her best shiny shoes. Very quietly, Karen opened her bedroom door. But there was her mum!

"Back to bed!" said Karen's mum.

Karen's lip wobbled and she started to cry.

Karen's mum put her arms round Karen.

"I do know how unhappy you are," said Karen's mum. "It feels like the end of the world, doesn't it? But we all get disappointed sometimes. It's part of life."

"It's not fair!" said Karen.

"I know," said her mum. "But it won't last. This afternoon you won't feel half so sad. I promise."

Karen's mum sat with Karen all morning. They did a jigsaw puzzle and read some books. Karen kept looking at the clock.
"They'll be taking the photographs now," she thought.

At lunchtime, Karen wasn't hungry. Her head still ached. Karen checked her face in the mirror – the lump on her neck was bigger!
"I look terrible," she said. Karen's mum gave her a hug.
"It could be worse," said Karen's mum. "Some people get two lumps with mumps." It sounded so funny that it made Karen giggle.

Marie came in to share the joke.

"I thought you were sad today," she said to Karen.

"I was – but it didn't last," said Karen. "I'm sorry I was nasty. Mumps isn't so bad after all."

How did Karen's mum help?

Who would you talk to, if you felt sad?

Feeling like Karen

Have you ever been disappointed, like Karen? Have you looked forward to going somewhere and then found that you couldn't go, after all? It makes you feel let down and sad. And you know that there is nothing you can do about it.

The end of the world

Everyone gets disappointed sometimes – adults too. And disappointments are always hard to take. But, as Karen's mum said, this kind of sadness doesn't last long. It's painful at the time, but the feeling soon goes. Remember that, when you're disappointed. Tell yourself that it's not the end of the world.

Talking about it

It's hard to be kind to others when you're feeling sad. You may seem cross or unfriendly. You may snap at people, as Karen did. And that often makes you feel worse. Try talking instead. If you tell your friends how bad you're feeling, they'll understand. It's good to have friends around when you're feeling sad.

Think about it

Read the stories in this book. Think about the people in the stories. Do you feel like them sometimes? What has made you unhappy? Think what you do when you're feeling sad. Think what is the best thing for you to do. Next time you feel sad, ask yourself these questions. Why am I sad? Is there a way to change things? Who is the best person to help me? Then talk to someone you trust.

Lee's story

Lee was standing in his bedroom. But there was no bed there, now. There were no cupboards, either – just four bare walls. Everything in Lee's room had been packed into boxes and stacked in a huge van. Lee's family was moving house.

Lee looked round his bedroom for the last time. Near the window there was a felt pen stain on the carpet. On the wall there were some marks where his football posters had been.

"I like this room," thought Lee.

Lee could hear someone calling him from downstairs.

"Lee-ee!" the voice echoed. But Lee didn't answer straight away.

"Goodbye, room!" he said out loud.

When Lee went downstairs, his friend Sam was there.

"I can't stay long," said Sam. "I'm on my way to the match."
Lee and Sam usually went to the match together.

Lee and Sam leaned against the kitchen door. Lee was very quiet. He didn't want to talk.

"I wonder what your new school will be like?" said Sam. "At least you won't have Mr Duffy for maths!"

"I'll let you know," said Lee quietly.

"I'd better go," said Sam. "See you, then, Lee."

"See you," said Lee.

Why didn't Lee feel like talking?

Lee sat down on the doorstep. He watched Sam cycle away. Lee felt awful. "Sam's my best friend," he thought. And Lee started to cry.

Lee's big brother Nathan sat down next to him. Nathan was fourteen and had a girlfriend. Nathan sighed.

"I just said goodbye to Sophie," said Nathan.

"I just said goodbye to Sam," said Lee.

Just then, Lee's dad came into the kitchen.

"Almost ready, boys," he said. "We're just waiting for your mum now." Lee and Nathan just nodded.

"Well, look at you two!" said Lee's dad.

"We don't want to move," said Lee.

"I know what you mean," said Lee's dad. "I'm feeling a bit sad too." Lee's dad looked round for somewhere to sit. But the room was empty. He sat down on the floor.

"What will you miss most?" he asked.

"Sophie," said Nathan.

"I'll miss Sam and my friends at school," said Lee.

"I'll miss this house," said Lee's dad. "And my friends at work. I've enjoyed living here."

What would you miss if you moved home
Would you feel sad too

"But I'm looking forward to our new home too," said Lee's dad. "Aren't you?"

Lee thought hard.

"Well, I'll like having a new maths teacher," he said.

"And I'll like having a new boss!" said Lee's dad.

"The new school sounds okay!" said Nathan.

"We can make lots of new friends!" said Lee.

"It's quite an adventure, isn't it?" said Lee's dad.

Then it was time to leave. Lee's mum was the last to get into the car.

"I'll really miss that house," she said sadly.

"Think of the new one!" said Nathan.

Lee's mum turned to the boys in the back seat.

"We can visit Sam and Sophie in the holidays," she said.

"And they can visit us," said Lee. "They can meet our new friends!"

How do you think Lee and Nathan are feeling now

What helped them to change their minds about moving

Feeling like Lee

Have you felt sad, like Lee? Have you ever moved to a new town, leaving your friends behind? Or perhaps a friend of yours has moved away? Losing a friend or leaving a neighbourhood can make you very unhappy. You think of all the good times that you've had. You know that things will never be the same again.

Thinking ahead

At times like this try to think ahead. Try to imagine making new friends. Or think of the fun you'll have exploring your new neighbourhood. You could make a list of all the things to look forward to. There are lots of good times on the way.

Ella's story

Ella's mum was busy. Ella could hear her banging around in the spare room. But she wasn't singing. And Ella's mum always sang while she worked. Something must be wrong.

"What are you doing, Mum?" asked Ella.

"I'm making up a bed," said Ella's mum. "Gran is coming to stay."

Ella's mum's eyes were red and Ella thought she was crying. Ella felt a little bit scared.

"Is Grandad coming too?" asked Ella. Ella's mum sat on the bed. She pulled Ella down next to her.

"Grandad is dead, Ella," said her mum quietly.

"Like Roly?" asked Ella. She remembered her furry little hamster, who had died last year.

"Yes," said Ella's mum, "just like Roly."

There were lots of things that Ella didn't understand. But her mum was talking again.

"I want you to be especially kind to Gran," said Ella's mum. "She's very upset, so you're not to bother her. And you're not to worry your dad, either." Ella nodded.

How is Ella feeling?

Then Ella's dad came home. He went into the kitchen with Ella's mum. They shut the door. But Ella could hear them talking. Ella wondered what they were saying. But she sat quietly and waited for Gran to come.

Soon the doorbell rang. Ella's dad rushed to answer the door. There was Gran. She looked very small and very old. Ella wanted to give her a big hug. But Ella's mum showed Gran straight upstairs.

"It's your bedtime, Ella," said Ella's dad.

"Can I go in to see gran first?" asked Ella.

"Not tonight," said her dad. "She's tired. And don't bother your mum, either."

Ella had lots of questions to ask. But she kissed her dad and went to bed.

What do you think Ella wanted to ask

What would you do now if you were Ella

Ella couldn't sleep. She was thinking about Grandad. She thought about his big, smiling face. And she remembered the way he always called her his "favourite little girl".

"I'll never see Grandad again," she thought. Ella felt very sad.

When Ella woke up it was early. She climbed out of bed and crept along to the spare room. The door was open, so Ella went in. Gran was sitting near the window.

"Mum and Dad told me not to bother you," said Ella.

"That's all right," said Gran. "Come and talk to me."

Ella snuggled into Gran's lap.

"Why did Grandad die?" she asked.

"When someone gets very old," said Gran, "their body just stops working – like a worn-out machine. That's what happened to Grandad."

"Did he say 'goodbye' to you?" asked Ella.

"No," said Gran. "He didn't have time."

Ella started to cry. "When I think about Grandad, I get a pain inside," she said.

"So do I," said Gran. "It hurts when someone you love dies. The pain will get better in time – just like a hurt leg. But you shouldn't pretend it isn't there."

"We'll never see Grandad again," said Ella.

"That's right," said Gran. "But we can remember him. We can talk about him and look at photographs. We can remember the things he used to say."

"So he's still around in some ways," said Ella. It made her feel much better.

When Ella's mum came in, Ella and Gran were still talking.
"I told Ella not to bother you," said Ella's mum, crossly.
"Ella's no bother," said Gran, smiling. "She's my favourite little girl."

How did Gran help Ella?
Do you think Ella helped her gran too?

Death is a fact of life

Death happens to everyone one day. It is a fact of life. Like Ella's mum, many people don't like to talk about death. They say it is a painful, sad subject. But it is important to think about it sometimes. Talking will help you to understand death. It will help you when someone you know dies.

Feeling like Ella

If someone you love dies, it leaves you feeling strange and lonely. You may feel sad for a long time. Like Ella, you may have lots of questions to ask. And at first you may not understand exactly what death means. You know that you will never see the person again. But you may not quite believe it. You may keep hoping that they will come back, although you know they can't.

Asking questions

When you're feeling sad, it helps to be with someone you know well. It helps if you tell them just how you feel. If you have any questions or worries, don't keep them inside. If the first person you tell doesn't want to talk, don't give up. Like Ella, make sure your questions are answered.

Feeling sad

Think about the stories in this book. Karen, Lee and Ella were each sad in different ways. And they each found someone to help them. If you say, "I'm sad," someone will help you too.

If you are feeling frightened or unhappy, don't keep it to yourself. Talk to an adult you can trust, like a parent or a teacher. If you feel really alone, you could telephone one of these offices. Remember, there is always someone who can help.

ChildLine
Freephone 0800 1111

The Line
ChildLine helpline for young people living away from home
Freephone 0800 884444
3.30pm to 9.30pm (weekdays)
2pm to 8pm (weekends)

NSPCC Child Protection Line
Phone 0808 800 5000

The Samaritans
Phone 08457 909090